For Tony Ogden and Nick Sanderson.

Not because you would ever need a book like this,
but because your spirit is embedded within its pages.

# This book belongs to:

___

# The Ballad of Skyfox

## Bob Stanley

*Top of the Pops* was my school. Drummers always looked like they were having the most fun to me and so, aged eight, I imagined myself as a drummer. A drummer in an invented pop group. In 1974, my fictional band was Skyfox, and I wrote their name on the white underside of my mum's circular tea tray. I had no idea it was meant to be a bass drum; to me, it was just the circular sign placed in front of the drummer proclaiming the name of the band.

There was no music involved in this fantasy, because it was much easier to come up with the exciting stuff around the edges. It worked in the same way that, as a kid, you can invent a country in your mind – the flag, the name of the capital, the football clubs – without having to worry about whether its utilities should be run centrally, or by county councils, or by unitary authorities.

Invariably, the first thing you thought of for your invented band was hair and clothes. And the band's logo, for the bass drum/tea tray. By the time you're at secondary school you might actually decide to play an instrument. I never made it to this stage.

Some kids at school looked like pop stars in waiting, but not many. Every afternoon I'd see this kid from another school at South Croydon station who looked vaguely American, a bit like a surly Leif Garrett but with David Cassidy's hair. This was 1977 and we'd have both been twelve or thirteen. He always removed his tie, and he never spoke to anyone. I could imagine him on stage with girls screaming, but I never heard any music when I pictured this. Just this kid mumbling into the microphone and the girls yelling. I also remember how he started putting on weight over a year until, by 1978, his shirt looked too tight and he began to develop a double chin. I didn't think he looked like a pop star after that.

We were spoilt for genuine pop stars in the seventies. Even beyond the obvious glam figures there were strange groups like the Doctors of Madness. And singers like Noosha Fox, who I assumed had tapped into my brain and abbreviated Skyfox to create her own (admittedly better) band name. These people lived in another world, where everything looked alien, quite different – a hundred times better than your world.

To get some idea of why you might want to be in a band, let's stay with Noosha Fox for a moment. In the nineties, someone told me that Noosha was running a restaurant in Oxford. Did I want to go? Of course I did. Did I know what kind of food it was? Couldn't care less. I didn't fancy Noosha Fox, I didn't care what kind of cuisine it was, I just assumed from her short-lived TV presence – Fox's hit run lasted just over a year – that it would be powerfully different in some way. That's what being in a band was about. Again, it had little to do with Fox's music. It was hard to explain. The nineties was still (just) pre-internet, and so I never went to Noosha Fox's restaurant because there was no way of finding the name or address. Googling in 2022 reveals it may have been an urban myth.

As a kid, I thought it was quite marvellous that Alvin Stardust had been Shane Fenton a decade earlier (everyone seemed to know this, even at the time). I couldn't understand why other pop stars thought he was somehow cheating. I couldn't make up my mind what I thought of David Bowie's form of shapeshifting, though, until 'Sound And Vision' came out and I loved its clean sleek tone that matched his new hair. When I was a bit older, the suburban, Kent-borders backdrop became my favourite thing about Bowie: his early, dashed attempts at making it in London; his sneaking back to Beckenham and re-inventing the backroom of a pub as the Beckenham Arts Lab, his home in a non-descript Victorian house called Haddon Hall, which photos suggested was a cross between a Ladbroke Grove squat and an abandoned chateau, when in reality it was a stone's throw from the none-more-commuter-belt Clock House station.

I loved Bowie's re-invention of the familiar and the banal. I could even relate, coming from the neighbouring London borough of Croydon. But what I couldn't do was re-invent myself. I couldn't, like his main mid-seventies rival Bryan Ferry, have pretended to have grown up a member of the landed gentry when in fact he was a part-time art teacher from a nothing town in County Durham. Not even Newcastle-upon-Tyne, like his bandmates, which at least had a smidgen of Likely Lads glamour. But the detail quickly becomes irrelevant if you act like you were born for the hunt, a scion of Castle Howard, a freakish cross between Gatsby and Prince Charles. The lie becomes reality. Many of Ferry's fans would turn against him, and convince themselves Brian Eno had invented and driven Roxy. This was also a lie.

Maybe I was scared of re-invention because it can be so dangerous. There's always the uncomfortable possibility that the required arrogance of a new look and a new name might mean you end up looking like Sting. He was a familiar figure to all of us, the new kid at school who gives himself a nickname and says it's what everyone at his old school called him. Most of these kids end up on the junkheap that Dexys sang about on the diptych of 'Show Me' and 'I'll Show You'. Some freaks like Sting or Bono somehow become rich and famous, unlicenced rock stars, but they could never be Bowie or even Ferry.

An alternative rock and pop route – which is vaguely the road I took – is to embrace a backroom role. This doesn't necessarily preclude mystique. In 1979 Alan Tarney wrote and produced 'We Don't Talk Anymore', the shiniest, most up-to-date and futuristic record of a year, which provided plenty of contenders. A few years later he took a morose trio of Norwegians, who made a calling card of their salt-and-pepper sandwich diet, and turned their song 'Take On Me' into an endless Pepsi fountain. Then after a few years away, he dabbled, just to show he still could, and turned Pulp's 'Disco 2000' from a middling album track into their most beloved hit. Then he disappeared. No one knows where he is now. No one even has a photo of Alan Tarney. I like that.

I'd like to say that reading this book put me off the idea of being a rock and pop star. I'd like to pretend there's a lot of work involved, too much work for me, and I'm just not interested. I'm happy with Skyfox as a figment of my imagination, rather than something I'd still like to enact. The truth is, I only ever had a temporary licence to rock and pop and it was revoked years ago.

**‘So, Wayne, when does the mind-bending start?’** Tony Ogden

**‘Look at me,
I am like you.’** Pierre Poujade

**‘I’ll be your mirror,
reflect what you are.’**

Lou Reed

# You Are Your Own Reaction

## Andrew Hunt

In August 2001, Earl Brutus, the band founded by Nick Sanderson and James Fry, performed as a living artwork at the Austrian Cultural Forum in London's Knightsbridge at an event organised by CRASH! (Matt Worley and Scott King). Just before the band went on stage to play three songs, including 'SAS And The Glam That Goes With It' – a number that contains the repeated chant 'You Are Your Own Reaction' – the Russian political artist Alexander Brener started to throw objects, trash the bar, and hurl abuse at King and Worley during their film screening in an attempt to bring the event to a close.

The reason for Brener's presence at the gallery was due to his and Barbara Shurz's exhibition at the venue that contained dozens of small text pieces drawn by hand in black marker pen that criticised key members of the British art world, part of the project 'Summer School of Bukaka'. Unfortunately, Brener had underestimated Earl Brutus and its wider circle's capacity for direct action. His measures were met with an immediate response, and he was swiftly and effortlessly 'punished' and dispensed with, as smoke bombs were detonated, and the band played on.

On 12 November 2001, three months after the antics described above, the first issue of *Slimvolume Poster*

*Publication* was launched in the form of a small show of A3 prints by thirty artists in the same exhibition space. The event was attended by such creative luminaries as artist Gustav Metzger, the collector Thomas Frangenberg, the curator and educator Teresa Gleadowe and writer Tom McCarthy (who prior to the 'Summer School of Bukaka' had presented a show by the International Necronautical Society as it's General Secretary). All had been nominated to receive copies of the full portfolio of works by the artists involved.

Importantly, the prints in the exhibition included a small Xerox copy of an original poster by Brener shown in August, which stated: 'State Violence is as English as … as … as … as … as … Pudding! …

it is for you dearest Matthew Higgs'. Higgs, who was present at the concert, had taken Brener's work from the exhibition, reproduced it, and placed a copy in the same spot from which it had been taken. Its new title, *You Are Your Own Reaction (after Alexander Brener for Scott King)*, formed a site-specific homage to this brief and chaotic event, which had immediately passed into the stuff of folklore.

Twenty years later, we can see this narrative within Fry's new book in a wider context of change. The looping sonic chaos and tragi-comic nature of Brener, King and Worley's CRASH! and Earl Brutus' escapades alongside Higgs' self-deprecating reflexivity provide a counterpoint to categories of contemporary conceptual appropriation, design, pop, glam, class and attitude in popular music, with the classic publication by communication theorist Marshall Mcluhan's *The Medium is the Massage* as its model. The period since 2001 has obviously seen a huge shift in culture, politics, and art, and with the two events mentioned above taking place just before and after 9/11 – the first resembling a terrorist attack in the embassy district of London, something passers-by and residents were concerned about at the time – we have subsequently seen the financial crisis of 2008, Brexit, Trump, #MeToo, Black Lives Matter, the Coronavirus Pandemic and the Russian invasion of Ukraine. With this shift, the subject of creative metamorphosis in music with a political or intelligent urgent edge has implications for the development of current cultural identities. If before 2001, risk-taking and transformation were very evident in pop, afterwards we might say that we have seen an increasingly careful, almost moral approach to personal revolution. Think Mumford and Sons and Coldplay.

A preference for fluid identities and a literary tradition exists in this book with an alternative history, that of the glittering indolence of Pater, Wilde, and Eliot – an imagined pole-vault over twentieth century critical theory – combined with the unlikely image of the dynamic Isambard Kingdom Brunel as the pre-eminent industrial post-woke pin-up. Forget Guy Debord, the Situationists and punk: Fry gives us the extreme anti-fashion of the under-represented and marginalised as the last great avant-gardes of the twentieth century. In line with this, Fry refers fondly to the actions of 2001, moments before police arrived and Earl Brutus finished their set on the first page of his introduction to this book…

# Introduction

> 'I was on stage, eggs and melons and glasses were being thrown at me. Nick, our singer, was shouting 'MALE MILK, SPREAD IT AROUND' down the microphone; he'd made a Sellotape impression of the British Rail logo on his jumper. Shinya was doing karate kicks in a puddle of lager as splinters of glass rained down on to our stage and into the audience. Meanwhile, a bloodied Russian conceptual artist was screaming and kicking over trestle tables in the distance.
>
> We had been sent here to destroy everything that we loved, and it felt good and it felt right. I couldn't hear myself think, I couldn't think, I felt like Bruce Lee, I was so happy. I knew I'd arrived. I knew it was over ... Now I was somebody.'
>
> You are your own reaction
> James Fry, 2022

James Fry made the transformation from spectator to spectacle as a founder member of the now legendary 'force of rock' that was Earl Brutus – still to this day regarded as a 'glam/electronic/neo-punk phenomena' that challenged the boundaries of taste and reached almost illegal levels of hysteria during their live appearances.

His adventures with The Pre New also makes a majestic connection with audiences across Europe, transmitting the band's warped, sometimes-corrupt perspective on the world, through the medium of radio, plastic, magnetic tape, and through the naked eye and naked ear.

James has always been a thoroughbred pop head. His privileged view of the world is the result of a journey that began by witnessing, at an early age, many of the masters of rock in his native Manchester.

He went on to observe his big brother 'transition' from an introspective sixth-former watching *Top of the Pops* on the family sofa, to a shiny gift-wrapped vocalist on that same television set in a matter of months, an excellent example of putting the 'U' and 'ER' into their collective name of Fry. All be it short-lived, James remembers this period as genuinely exciting, shocking and instantaneous.

He played an integral part in the post-baggy Manchester orbit as a photographer and lighting director to his closest allies, Gordon, Tony and Nick, AKA World of Twist, who 'successfully left their stain on British pop culture'. Their only album cover, which Fry photographed, would go on to win the 1991 Worst Record Cover of the Year in *The Independent* newspaper.

James has also photographed enough shite bands to know what he is on about.

He continues to this day to excavate, exhume and generate vibrant and arresting imagery as an art director, archive producer, editor and photographer.

This book is a direct reaction to all of those experiences, and more. Written from his own unique perspective, it is, as James readily admits, 'from the heart'.

And throughout this journey he has produced an endless photographic record of pop and rock's best and worst.

# How This Book Works

### This book is an antenna

It receives and transmits popular culture and the visual language of rock and pop from the current landscape, amplifying the signals it receives back into the space it occupies, asking questions, and offering reaction and understanding.

The process of realising this publication has been achieved in an extremely natural and organic form. None of the following pieces of writing pretend to deal with more than our own personal responses to popular music. In essence, it presents cause and effect and is thus designed to provoke a polarised response from the viewer/reader.

### This book is a manual

On how to embrace the courage required to become a first-class spectacle. It recognises the techniques and crafts of others and aims to demonstrate how to process them though one's own personality. Such an approach allows the user to express oneself successfully and to better appreciate the codes and actions of those whom history has marked out as celebrated performers.

### This is a self help book

It offers the reader an alternative to spending their life as a passive observer, offering them the confidence and self-belief to stand defiant on stage. Imagine one last time that you are a spectator. Read and understand this little publication and it will be impossible for you to ever imagine such a thing again. This guide will completely change the way that you feel about yourself as an audience member forever.

**This book ends with a questionnaire**

Within this comprehensive manual, there is a series of text/image and image-only chapters that provide the reader with definite answers with which to aid the successful completion of the questionnaire at the end of the compendium. Each section naturally takes something of a blinkered view on its given subject, yet clearly defines the manual's intention to encourage a process of questioning. It is the natural and instinctive response of the reader that will be audited, and this response will then be measured to enable a successful application for a licence.

**This book is an inventory of attitude.**

# The Licence Completion Procedure

Read carefully through this book, one chapter at a time, in chronological order.

**Do not under any circumstances read each chapter outside of their natural order.** This may compromise your successful application for a licence.

Once you have completed reading this book, please complete the attached licence request application. This form can be found at the back of the guide. Applications should be written clearly in block capitals, in black ink, avoiding mistakes. (Further copies of the application form can be downloaded from www.slimvolume.org)

Please send completed and signed forms, along with an A4 stamped address envelope to the book's publisher, Slimvolume.

You should receive a reply within twenty-eight days of posting your application. Should you fail in the first instance, you can re-apply for your licence as many times as you wish, however any cross-referencing will be taken into account and may affect the auditor's final decision.

Good luck,
James Fry

# Chapter 1

## Stance + Ego = Showing Off

The stance of the performer and his/her presence in/on a magazine, record sleeve, website or stage, and at all the times within the viewers' gaze, is forever important. Without the necessary posture, the artist will never have the will or charisma to appear before an audience and be worshipped.

Stance is as important as ego. Without an absurdly high-level of hunger to 'show off', it is impossible to make the audience wet with desire.

A good performer can do this with a flick of the wrist; a truly great performer will do it with a flick of his/her cock/cunt.

Once mastered, the noble art of showing off (and it truly *is* a noble art) can generate hysteria in its purest form. The skilled performer understands this, and as a result, will work the audience down to their knees. He/she can generate an electrical charge that will connect with the spectator's head, heart, spine and genitalia.

Men, women and cameras will love the 'star' forever; boys will want to be with it (and have sex with it); girls will want to have sex with it (and own it). The camera aches to have it in its gaze and craves to record its image…

…meanwhile, up on the higher ground, the performer performs. A play to the back of the hall and to the front row, to the lights and the shadows, to the microphone and the wires…it's all so natural…without sparing a thought for the audience. After all…it does all of this for no one but itself…a gratuitous and selfish act.

After all…does the audience really deserve to be in the presence of a super-mortal?

After all…aren't they simply workers with well-paid bad jobs?

Consider this image of Isambard Kingdom Brunel (IKB). It is clearly one of the most important photographs of the nineteenth century. An icon and a fashion photograph in the truest sense.

IKB's top hat helps him read as a man of class, vision and authority. He is not an everyman. He is not a pensions adviser from Harrogate. He is better than you.

Now consider the cigar. It is not simply a tool for generating smoke, but an extension of the penis.

This phallic radar reaches out into the viewers' gaze and redirects them to a lower place. (Other examples include Clint Eastwood and Winston Churchill, both of whom clearly admired this photograph.)

Mud on boots – obviously IKB was one of the boys. You just know these boots could stand alone and tell their own story. Their owner is not afraid of hard work, of mucking in and getting dirty. They/he lead/s by example.

Stance: Brunel's key contribution to this image is his stance. His sense of well-being and confidence binds the ingredients together.

In this chain of visual signifiers:

**Work**
**=**
**Dirt**
**=**
**Cash**
**=**
**Success**
**=**
**Power.**

Background: Other forces are at play in this photograph. Particularly through its use of background. The oversized chain at the rear of the image, for example, tells us a great deal about the subject it supports. The huge links suggest a dockside or ship just out of view and, in turn, conveys an image of a man who is more than just a run-of-the-(satanic)-mill industrialist. This man is in the big league. He is a powerful presence in the industrial revolution public relations arena. The chains carry with them a sub-plot that is almost homoerotic in its majesty, a super-power metaphor that frames the image and sustains the viewer's gaze beyond IKB. Indeed, this is a metaphor that suggests a 'more than human' heroic species, an unforgettable vision recycled and reproduced way beyond its years.

It has been argued that the image on
the following page is the most important
photograph of the twentieth century.

From its first viewing, this photograph has been regarded as both a monolithic statement and a hard comment on attitude and visual couture.

This 'group' have an advantage over IKB. They have each other to play off against. Strong vs. weak, tall vs. small, found control vs. lost control.

The image would have been weaker had it not be so uniform and strong. The group's choice of attire presents the notion of a common goal. All for one and one for all. The text above their heads confirms this.

This is a typical family portrait, loaded with the equilibrium of everyday life. Secure on the outside, a complex set of torrid emotions within.

The four individuals within the captured image suggest rebellion and revolution. The group or band represent all the conventions of the renegade or repeat offender. However, the four individuals are essentially four different facets of IKB's own posture and excitement. These figures are simply unused frames from the imaginary contact sheet on IKB's agent's desk, images that never made the final edit. Attitude, posture, adventure, even romance, all play a part as the four boys from New York City frame their legacy.

Again, the background is essential. It invites the viewer to consider the group's cultural boundaries. This time we see a tumble-down brick wall, a setting and an environment for the lost and alone, the poor, the immigrant or the disenfranchised. Housing estates, projects, bomb-sites and ghettos. This particular quartet choose to suggest the harsh inner-city as their canvas. This is a political climate without politics. It is their habitual launch-pad. Because of this: Johnny, Joey, Dee Dee and Tommy, we salute you.

'The boys', as we now know them, are an iconic example of I. K. Brunelism. They are a facsimile of his original. The boys are students of IKB's school. With hands in pockets and an excellent use of dark glasses (figure, right) during daylight hours, the boy's eyes are hidden alongside his true identity.

Although it is the boy on the left who is the original self-confessed 'punk' (New York street slang for male prostitute), the pair are friends, they share the same set of signals and notions, and they are one.

One foot raised* suggests a single beat.
Music is present in this photograph.

*This signifier works in the same simple manner as IKB's boots.
It suggests a great deal without really saying anything at all.

The worn jeans of the former punk/rent boy suggest that he has spent a large amount of time on his knees servicing a client. Whether this is actually the case is not made clear, adding intrigue and a little frisson of tension to the image.

Leg posture and correct positioning provides balance and function within any composition …

**at any angle**

and

from

any

viewpoint.

Common threads transcend centuries, where posture and gesture are portrayed in their purest form. It is also possible to reverse this description when analysing the art of dramatic pose.

The two images on the following page (Caravaggio/Bowie) emphasise this when placed side by side. Both central figures contain brave and destructive acts for the benefit of the viewer, and utilise their supporting cast in a powerful claim for drama.

To see Mick Rock's effortlessly powerful live photography set beside Caravaggio's masterpiece is to almost look at one singular image connected across the centuries, it's as if the painter is hearing the photographer's call from the future. Credit: Mick Rock

Silhouettes and shadows,
watch the revolution
No more free steps to heaven
Just walkie-talkie –
heaven or hearth
Just big heads and drums –
full speed and pagan
And it's no game

I am barred from the event
I really don't understand
the situation
So where's the moral
People have their fingers broken
To be insulted by these fascists
it's so degrading
And it's no game

Documentaries on refugees,
couples 'gainst the target
Throw a rock against the road,
and it breaks into pieces
Draw the blinds on yesterday,
and it's all so much scarier
Put a bullet in my brain,
and it makes all the papers
And it's no game

Children round the world,
put camel shit on the walls
They're making carpets
on treadmills,
or garbage sorting
And it's no game.

 'It's No Game, Part 2', David Bowie, 1980.

Contrary to tradition, Caravaggio depicts the moment before flagellation... as Jesus is tied to the column. Yanked and shoved into place, he stumbles into a graceful pose that is at once heroic, august and beautiful.

Pitting Christ's transcendent acquiescence against the raw brutality of his assailants, Caravaggio creates an image of arresting pathos. Stark light emphasises the strong presence of each figure as darkness weighs down upon the action. A lone column anchors the composition. A complex, balanced geometry of interlocking posture and attitude, each clearly studied from life, each separating light from darkness.

The last breaths of the lead performer are witnessed. On the left, a member of the group lies dead, while our hero tries one last time to fend off danger to protect those who were loyal to him. The character on the right moves away from this band of brothers, considering his own safety over his leader's fate. Seconds later, those who betrayed and killed the harmony of the group will move away and on into a future that ends with just one winner.

**Caught within the eye of a human tornado there is nothing he can do but simply wait to die.**

The battle of earth and the higher ground is once again acted out in the following image. Those who adore the idol will ultimately be responsible for his downfall, as they engulf and take what they need from him. In this feeding frenzy, a transition of power takes place. The force and light of the performer is drained from him, as his followers and believers become his destroyers.

**Caught within the eye of a human tornado there is nothing he can do but simply wait to die.**

The Icelandic rock God offers the viewer not just his groin, but a lifestyle beyond our natural reach. While his extremities remain wide open, his co-workers disassemble the tools of his trade on his behalf, because he has no time for the realities of life. His sexual essence transcends all reality.

Here, the older American lady allows us access to her extremities for a limited time. Her right leg is given as a peace offering to draw our attention away from the fact that the instrument that she holds adds very little to the action. Through gritted teeth, she is in control, wearing a top hat to prove her authority and secure her place in history, in the same manner as IKB.

'Look at you, you're all in my hands!', screams the star from the pages of this book. 'I, rock star. My limbs are spread so that I resemble a star. I am a star because I am star-shaped. I play rock. I am shaped like a star.'

Comparisons of the two accompanying images can remind the spectator that a simple composition of five, or even six people can be posed to have the same visual impact as a city's dominant sky line. When individuals come together as one, it is vital that they understand their relationship with one another and the impact they can have as a group.

To the viewer, this can signify adventure, anticipation and a sense of being. In short, a beautifully constructed group photograph is a human postcard that reads 'wish you were here'.

The individual is no longer important, the group is greater than the sum of its parts, much as lone buildings can seem bland and innocuous until placed alongside others to become a city, or the combination of five different flavours become a delicious meal.

WALKERS
NEW

WALKERS
CRISPS
IS THERE A SPICY
£100,000

WALKERS
CRISPS
Onion Flavour
IS THERE A SPICY

The pose of this solo gentleman holds a sense of poise with a dignity that is almost architectural in structure. The image is reminiscent of an IKB suspension bridge, the perfect construction of stability and balance. His surrounding everyday props explain that this is a man who truly enjoys the very best that life has to offer. International wine (travel and wisdom), a single glass (mystery and ambiguity) and amphetamine sulphate (virility).

This group
of individuals have
their genitals retouched
and flattened to emphasise a new
sexuality. They choose to avoid the
compartmental trappings of gender or
bourgeois concepts of fixed identity by refusing
to adhere to either 'male' or 'female'. This is an
act of defiance against their own peer group and
all that surround them, a form of insubordination
that is emphasised by their posture: chins in the
air, outward they stare, hands on hips. This
gender-fluid group evolve from a different
tradition. With their misbegotten
countenance they resemble the
'gloriously ugly'.

**Clever showmen showwomen showpeople understand themselves**: ugliness is part of the make-up.

This beatific arrogance suggests to the viewer that he/she/they are gazing with an otherworldly presence from a far off erotic and distant land. This nudity brands the performer.

Caught for a seismic second on a wide angle lens, embracing the nature of the woodland that surrounds them, this image isn't about nature, it is nature.

# Chapter 2

## Spectrum of Rock

# And . . .

yes

me.

# Chapter 3

## Self-Belief and Going Solo

We should now look at the ways in which solo artistry can have an even greater impact on the public.

As the examples on pages 88, 90 and 92 show us, once the balance of power within a group has been established, it will inevitably be overturned as natural patterns of ego and self-belief evolve.

History has always recognised the soloist. Luck, it is said, favours the brave. And it is those who have the courage to go it alone that will hold the key to ultimate power. They become an impenetrable force of freedom, because alone, as one, there is nothing to divide or destroy.

This is not always easy to achieve, nor is it particularly pleasant, but once it is within your grasp you can find yourself in a very special place with some very special friends. In Your Universe with others in Your Orbit, not you in theirs.

**Do you now have the confidence to go it alone, to become that indestructible solo performer?**

The next group of images depict insurmountable acts of self-belief that some readers may find disturbing.

# I get happiness from my

# dejection

# How lonely sits the city

**that was full of people**

The performer believes in 'him' and only in 'him'. This picture best describes the confidence one can achieve when self-respect is at its most powerful. Reproduced in duplicate for ultimate effect, the figure has no time for the camera; he is alone, unaware that he is pure spectacle. His mind is in a special place. His body is stretched to occupy as much of the world as possible because he believes that the more space he and his image occupy, the better the world will be.

He wears very little because he has no time for fashion. He is fashion. He simply wants to be a wonderful human being who contributes wholly to society while here on earth. He too, is star shaped.

The figure below has just finished work. He relaxes by the roadside, contemplating what he should do with the spare time he now has at his disposal. The image depicts a point in time where he has placed his microphone down (the tool of his trade) and is about to pick up a bottle of beer (a symbol of relaxation). He can put his feet up knowing that he has achieved a great deal on this day. He is fully aware that he always does what he wants, when he likes, wearing what he chooses. His interest is in instilling his art in noble people … not in plebeians. In every difficult, worthwhile endeavour, there will come a point when the easiest course of action is to abandon forward motion, to allow inertia to take over and to return to the status quo. It is the brave and great man who, upon recognising this point, resists inertia and smashes on through to the other side, no matter the cost.

We call this juncture 'the critical moment of will'.

This man has the ego and self-confidence to do this. This is because this man is in control and answers only to himself and no one else. He is 'a great guy'.

The figure on this page offers us his image. It is his gift to us. The gift is something we never thought we wanted or needed, until it was presented to us. Now we crave it. This is a picture of a man taken by himself. Within the image an outrageous act of self-belief is at play, as he offers us his own self-image covered in other images of himself, taken by him.

There is no space in the photograph for anyone else. The man's ego is far too momentous to accommodate anything other than himself. And, if this is not enough to define his self-belief, he places the camera at his own waist height and looks down on the viewer with his chin pointing upwards as a fierce act of self-confidence. We are here to serve him because this picture says so.

If you fail in world domination then you can always pretend. It has been said that if you lie enough then the lie will eventually become true. This is another, slightly uncomfortable but functional route to individual success, as the next image explains.

**The figure in the picture unquestionably has delusions of grandeur.** The image depicts his first homecoming back to his native London in many years. He has travelled the world with homes in the US and Germany (Berlin), and now returns to a hero's welcome. He receives his followers dressed in an informal black shirt and dark trousers, the leisure wear of the Nazi party. On the surface, this is a foolish and misguided act, a celebration of the moment when German troops invaded Britain during the Second World War. He is depicting a part of a history that never actually happened, but as a result, is deliberately addressing a sensitivity

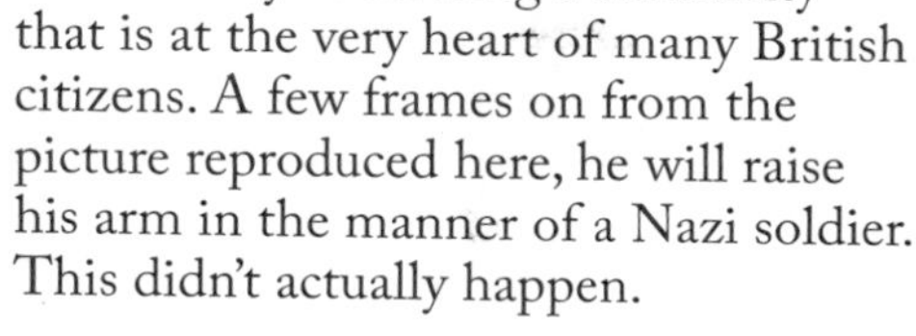

that is at the very heart of many British citizens. A few frames on from the picture reproduced here, he will raise his arm in the manner of a Nazi soldier. This didn't actually happen.

As an act of sheer confidence, the performer lets us think that it happened by supplying us with *nearly* all of the signifiers that we need to reconstruct the original act. He paints this picture using our imagination. He is not at fault, he only suggests that the act has taken place and, as a result, isolates himself and polarises the audience into two sections: those who despise him and those who admire him.

He now dispenses with the former and leads the latter into a more defined and optimistic future. Tomorrow belongs to him.

Make the next step to world domination by performing a similar act and you will have the power that others can only dream of obtaining…a future.

**Tomorrow belongs to you.**

# Here is a picture of God.

**The Lord God formed man from the dust of the earth. He blew into his nostrils the breath of life, and man became a living being.**

Genesis 2:7

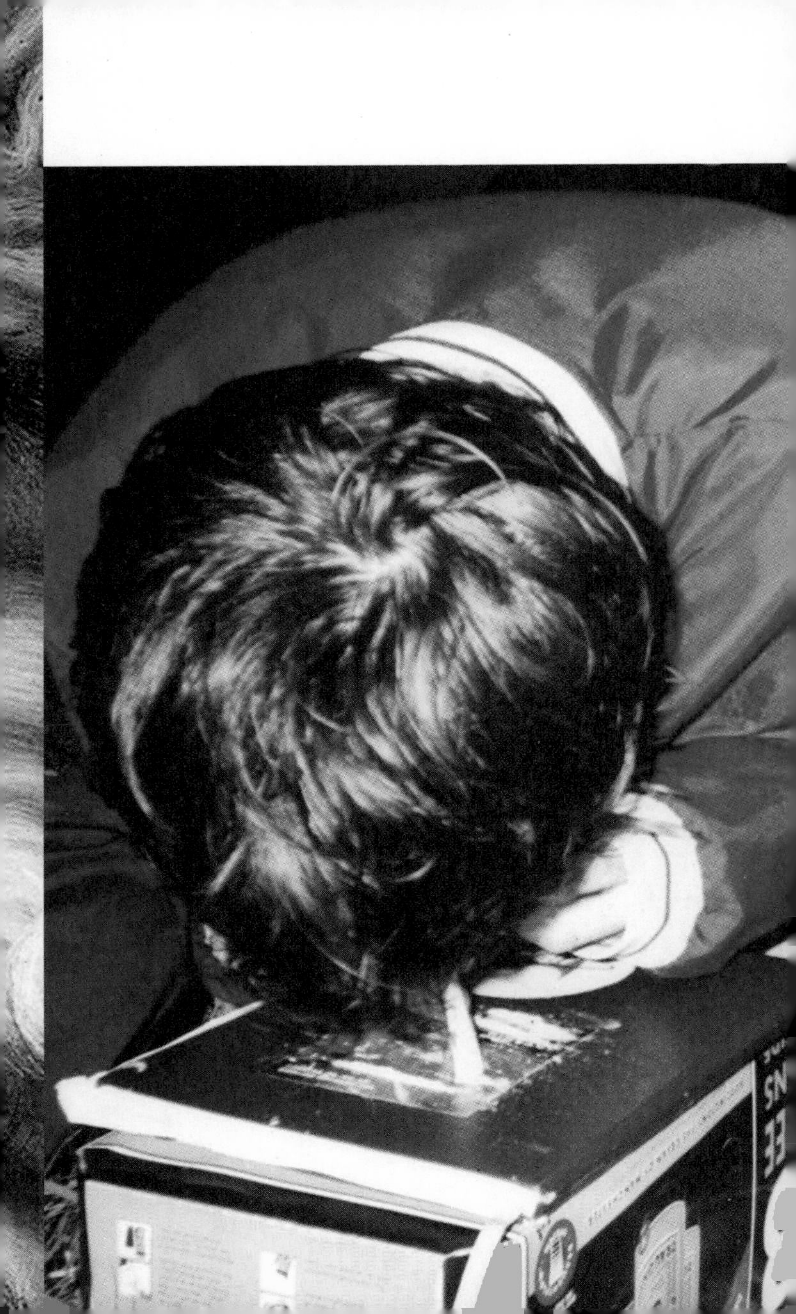

## These grown men are taking cocaine.

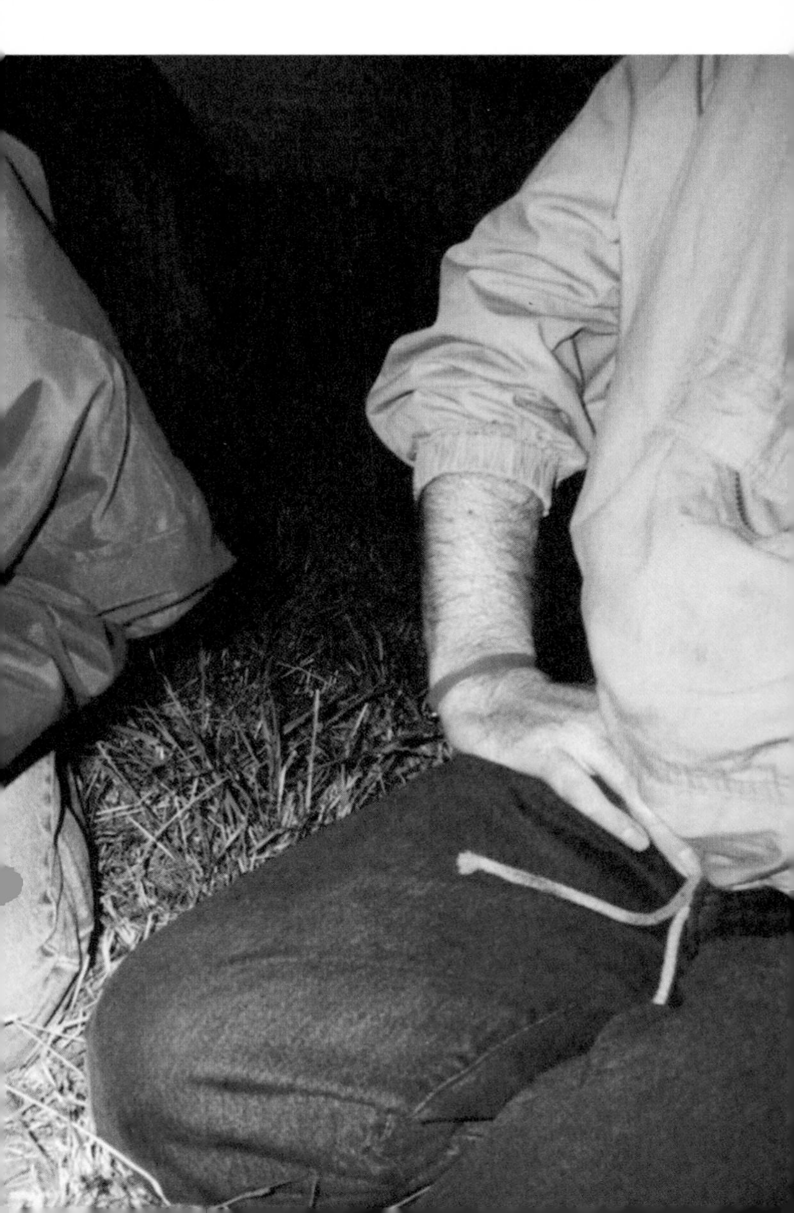

hapter 4

# How to Take Drugs

The 'Now' generation are a grim lot.

The 'Now' generation do not believe in drugs …

they are wrong.

These grown men taking drugs will very soon become intoxicated by their chosen chemical compound. They will subsequently feel like better people. This will be fundamental to their (rock) experience. Their imaginations will absorb their surroundings in a more receptive nature. The environment they are in will seem more saturated than it actually is. In their minds, they will appear to engage better with each other, while their milieu will appear to want them and love them. They will enter a 'New Reality'.

As their blood streams and brain cells react to their chosen chemical compound, they will feel **superior** and **God-like**.

Music will seem louder and more in tune. They will feel more liked than they actually are, the space that they occupy will appear bigger and more welcoming to their attitudes and ideals. We shall refer to this place as the 'Higher Ground'.

Drugs are the perfect tool for the spectator embarking on a journey toward spectacle for they convince him/her that they are better than they actually are. They assist in an ascension to the stage. They are sturdy props. However, it is as if this prop is made of ice or chocolate: drugs have a short life span and their effects soon melt away. But before they do, drugs offer strong belief without challenge. They are both tightrope and safety net, good Mother and bad Father. In short, drugs are simultaneously good and evil, providing false faith like nothing else on earth.

The old belief that hard work is rewarded with success is no longer relevant. This set of values no longer exists. The great-great-great-great-great-great-grandchildren of the people who invented this notion are now taking drugs to succeed.

It has been proven that attitude, not talent, is the fast lane to success and that, with drugs, one doesn't even need attitude. In fact, one can obtain victory and greatness though continued drug use alone. Moreover, this essential tool comes cheap. It is a bargain that enables one to float serenely in the space between satisfaction and God-like genius. Caravaggio would be jealous.

Drugs may be considered a joke, or even destructive among the ordinaries. It is said that they have destroyed relationships, families and unwanted jobs. However, this is a minor consideration when embarking on a journey towards the higher ground.

Some people are on fire, some have lost their fire and some others never had it in the first place.

Pass me the lighter.

Drugs are the journey. Everything else is roadside cafés and ugly hitchhikers.

It is this stretch upon the personality that aids the performer and spectacle. The high and the low. The ability to shift from one parameter to the other is the essence of the great performer. The personality becomes hollow in the centre, with all emphasis being placed on surface extremes, which are at breaking point. Like a colossal Easter egg without a yoke, weight is placed on pure surface, a lightbulb-like vacuum that enables the star to shine. The individual develops a less human form, becoming a paradox, a series of polar opposites.

This is 'the butterfly complex'. The star functions purely as decoration or jewellery. Although beautiful, this is ultimately a useless, indolent and short-lived form of existence. It carries with it its own destruction.

By placing the spectacle in a confined space, on a stage or in a glass box, to be observed in a so-called 'Big Brother' situation, the drug user's reaction can become extreme, as the diagram below shows:

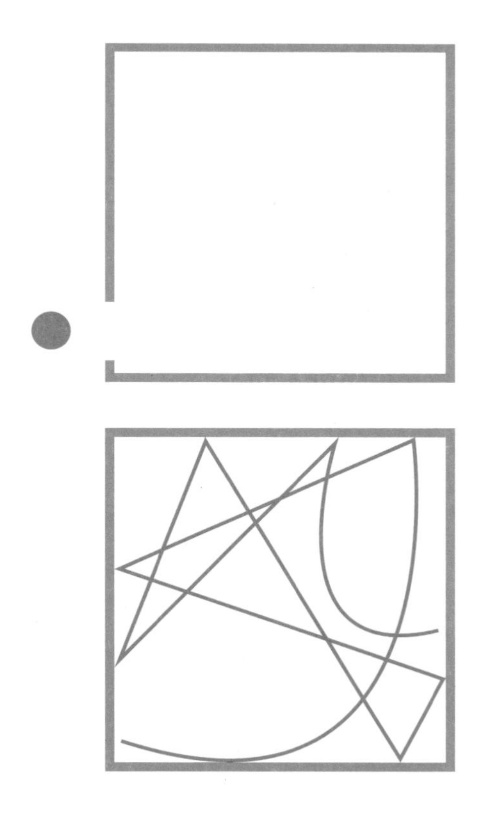

Remember, within this context: drugs are not necessarily a bad thing. The stronger the drug and the larger the amounts consumed, the more intense the personality becomes and, in turn, the brighter the spectacle appears to be.

Does the public want to see their own likeness? No. They want to see an exaggerated spectre of themselves in the most severe circumstances. A savage and splintered replica of themselves that acts out their wildest dreams and fantasies. This is a place on the very edge of personality. But it is a place that only the performer dares to go. A place where the frayed embers of the mind resides. Instead of persona, there exists a series of codes and signals that lash out in the dark, without rationale, where nothing and everything matters simultaneously. Meanwhile, tens of thousands, even millions of spectators, hold you in awe.

Drugs are cheap ... this is fast-tracking at its most extreme. At its fastest even, and even faster.

**This book belongs to:**

______________________________

# This

is

# How

# We

# Act

# Chapter 5

A new generation understands that putting a wide lens on a camera and filming in slow motion, or in black and white monochrome, leads to a recognised art form. This is an insecure and tired doctrine that no longer serves to provide any sense of time and place.

The importance of the location you lay claim to must never be underestimated. Your sense of time and place is the bedrock of your identity. It is on these foundations that all of your art will be hung. Don't make this a dull place.

For example, suburbia is a place where anything can happen and usually doesn't. Make it happen. What you choose to project onto the spectator is completely your choice. Pretend to turn your back on the place that once supported you, providing you with a safe haven away from the cruelty of the city. Claim that the city is now yours, and that you own it.

Once you were a young estate agent who caused petty mayhem at the weekend. Now you are a fully-fledged hooligan, seven days a week.

Once you have harboured your parent's money – having been ferried around in their Volvo estate for your teenage years – reject your secure reality and start lying.

As long as your untruth or invented reality comes from an extreme position on the social spectrum, it will generally work, however it's important to mention that this social spectrum or class reality is a self-generating loop (see images on preceding pages). The basic rule of thumb is to go against the grain of whatever is in vogue at the time.

Claiming that you are from the gutter will give you the sympathy vote. It has long been a popular choice. Acting the persecuted, introverted intellectual will generate further consideration and support. If you can subsequently prove that these claims are actually true, a place in the pantheon of greatness is guaranteed.

Once your identity and background have been created and established, make it very clear who you are not. We are all aware that the 'Jack-the-lad working-class' type makes a great 'scally with a heart'. Or that the 'introverted council estate boy fresh from returning his Nietzsche books to the local library' makes a spectacular 'victim-bites-back slacker/shoe-gazer lost-son'.

Understand that playing social games can send out a clear and substantial signal.

In essence, you should treat your own people with the contempt that they deserve in order to create distance. After all, you know more about them than you know about yourself. You are one of them, and once again, you are your own reaction.

Consider your upbringing for a moment. Take an honest look at how you were brought up during your formative years, and the time that you were cut loose from your parents or carers' ways of thinking, perhaps through death, deceit or boredom. This was a period when the world branded you emotionally, sexually, physically and cerebrally. Your personality and character were moulded into the person that you were going to be forever…

Now, change it. Make assumptions and dream up a new set of values. What do you consider to be an ideal upbringing that would be effective in resonating with your ideal fan?

Your choice should be instinctive and have no rational measure in terms of wealth or upward mobility. Where would you like to be in the heads of your followers? Are you a member of the working-class looking to own a stately home? Are you from the middle or upper classes, craving a heroin-soaked jazz existence in a project scheme or tower block? Are you city-based and urban to the core, longing to be propped up by the five-bar gate of your mind, drinking wine, refined? Are you black and longing to be white? Or are you white with a dyslexic black soul, desperate to express yourself politically, fashionably and socially? Will you wear your peaked cap backwards or forwards? Which way will you press your Levis?

Regardless of what those before you have claimed, this is an essential tool in the laws of presence and attitude. Remember, whatever signal you may choose to convey, it must be of a romantic nature. As some of the following images will explain, you are now at the core of twenty-first century living.

# ‘I am the leader of the gang!’ ...

… shouts the Fidel Castro-like figure in the centre of this frame, as his four friends look on. He wears clothes a lighter shade than his companions, to stand out against them. Their environment is the high seas. It's clear that these five men are high achievers and pioneers of their craft, as they navigate tempestuous winds, trading on the stock market of romance and adventure. Unlike our four boys from New York City, these men are clearly not 'rough trade'. Instead they offer a way out: 'I joined the rat race, and I won!' screams our hero.

This artist chooses the historical form of the nude – the unclothed human figure, an enduring tradition in Western art – to portray an otherworldly self-portrait. Essentially a depiction of flesh, the figure appears naked. When we look closer, however, we see a crucifix around his neck. Such an adornment reminds us that this man is a man of God and that, although he appears naked, he is a mortal on God's own earth and therefore not gratuitously naked, but simply as God created him. This image applies similar rules of representation to those found in the work of Michelangelo and Rubens.

PRINCE
LOVESEXY

This adult is the product of the street that he occupies, with the image signalling that these are the streets in which this man was raised. Wearing jeans and a jacket suggests that he has dignity and harbours a resentment of conformity. The shop that frames the two figures sells second-hand merchandise, intimating that the photograph echoes a mythical past.

By utilising a child in this picture, the viewer is led to believe that the adult is an 'all right kind of bloke' with a future. This image claims that the youngster looks forward to the day when he can be an adult. 'When I grow up, I want to be you!', he cries.

COME AND LOOK ROUND
STAGE + T.V SPECIALITIES
LARGE SIZES AVAILABLE
LOTS OF JACKETS TROUSERS, SHOES, RAINCOATS ETC ETC
SUITS !! 38-50 FROM £10
LEATHER SHEEPSKIN
SIZES
WOOLWORTH
ROOMS
IAN DURY NEW BOOTS AND PANTIES !!

These five men have made the journey down from the north of England – from downbeat, three-bedroom post-war universal-plan council-accommodation – via Concorde, to a fourteen-bedroom, home-counties mansion with pool (with car in pool, with girls in car, and with cocaine in girls).

They have a set of values, largely forged in the 1960s and 1970s, that they want us to consider. For example, they choose to squander the expensive motorcar but save the low-cost moped. How will they all get home? Do they live in the mansion?

oasis
AUGUST
21
THURSDAY
SYD 724F
514 FMK

These four individuals do not create a greater figure than the sum of their parts. They break the rebel gang rule with their individual characteristics, which ultimately make them more rebellious. They are four fathers who have all had a single child with the same woman. She enjoys herself. They don't enjoy themselves. They don't even like each other. However they are part of the same group. The point at which this picture was taken is as close as these men are ever going to get to each other. The image is stronger as a result.

The backdrop is passive in comparison to previous examples, which makes the separate elements far stronger. The turbulent estuary air is their swimming pool or brick wall. In the distance, a jetty suggests a point of departure and the possibility of a better place. These four young men are down, but have not been defeated by the harsh wind. They are the most positive people in the pages of this book so far.

Dr. Feelgood
Down By The Jetty

New York Dolls
© 1973 Phonogram, Inc.
mercury

Stereo SRM-1-675

These five individuals appear to be relaxing at home during a break after playing pop music, perhaps taking some drugs before meeting their record company.

But are they really individuals? This image offers the viewer the ultimate 'gang' experience because they choose to define themselves as a singular object (a band) though costume and make-up across a fluid gender spectrum.

It's hard not to discuss this visual construction without considering the climate that this photograph was born into, a time of macho rock and American conservatism. This gang offer themselves up for sacrificial attack from a narrow and unsympathetic public.

This was a battle cry and a declaration of war for the next generation to embrace. However, in the present, to a McCarthy-instilled cautious Victorian public, this image is impossible to place.

This image does not portray the beginning or end point of any activity. It is a mere moment in time before the five-piece disperses the scene. For now, they are moving in one direction.

This is a domestic image. In this simple document, we glimpse the lives and styles of the individuals of a typical family, choosing the most natural definitions of family life, the sofa, to present themselves to us, the viewer.

Nothing is staged, everyone here is in their natural default position.

The enigmatic figure on the far left appears to be a character in this story that will stay put, at home. A quiet night in, watching television perhaps? A glass of prosecco? Another cigarette maybe?

Moving left to right, the next figure portrays a paradox of stasis and mobility in a single pose. More than any other, his roller-skates will take him far from this domestic scene, perhaps to a 1970s roller disco, or simply for a roll around The Lower East Side. The sofa may offer the security of a nest, but this creature has metaphorical 'wings'.

The central figure pushes out from the framework of this traditional family portrait and displays unprecedented ambition and intent. His high heels and posture represents a desire for a greater attitude and a higher altitude than his colleagues. This suggests that, for now, he has dispensed with this particular faux-family tableau, as he gets ready for his next adventure, pruning and pouting with the use of a small compact mirror, which occupies his thoughts entirely. Abject beauty is offered here, together with a possible sexual encounter with oneself. He doesn't have to share the mirror with anyone else just yet. Arrogance is also present. This individual has no need for roller-skates or any other form of transportation because he will obviously be chauffeured into the next scene at no cost.

In white platform boots, white belt and embroidered shirt reminiscent of the American Wild West – a fictitious place where men were represented by an absolute form of masculinity, while femininity was merely a background feature – this wild west doll wears makeup and teases his hair in a provocatively feminine fashion. This player chooses not to drink from a glass. Instead, with legs wide open, he swallows directly from a can of beer in the language of the butch. This particular doll manages to be the most masculine of this group. His choices carry a dark elegance. He is the dark horse. He is a paradox of sexual codes that is simultaneously unapproachable and welcoming.

By contrast, the most elegant and respectable doll can be found on the far right of this scene. Determined to escape this setting and join another more respectable party – not with force, but with gentle charm – his beauty is our beauty. Hands clasped together like a school headmistress, his back faces the group, suggesting that he wishes to throw himself clear of this family and better himself.

He considers himself better than them. He
gazes into his future and considers his next move.
He imagines leaving all of this vulgarity behind.
His plan is to confront issues of penis envy and
castration anxiety in a more spectacular manner
in order to 'spice up his life'.

In this image, the artists choose to allow possessions to represent themselves in the public eye. This is a powerful statement within the structure of class, and is far less complex than the preceding pictures. This photograph sends only one signifier to the viewer's gaze: wealth.

Nevertheless, by placing this image into the public arena they have given their own possessions higher status than themselves. This could be a brave and political statement about where they are from and where they are now. Or it could be a means of hiding from the public eye, due to issues of low self-esteem and a wish to remain anonymous. Since there are no people in this image for the viewer to identify with, and no central iconic prop within the composition, emphasis is placed on text placed across the top of the frame.[†]

† Amongst the credits that accompany the original image it is not only the photographer who is named, but also the jeweller/goldsmith.

The Love Unlimited Orchestra
White Gold
STEREO
T-407
1. STANDING IN THE SHADOWS OF LOVE 5:00
2. BRING BACK MY YESTERDAY 4:40
Arranged by Barry White & Gene Page
A SOUL UNLIMITED PRODUCTION

Similarly, the practitioners or band behind this photograph choose to remain anonymous. Instead, other symbols of liberation and sexual politics are framed. The two women in the image are caught in the headlights of a passing car. They were previously hiding in the bushes behind them. What were they doing there? This picture is loaded with powerful innuendo. It is soft porn after a sexual event has taken place. The background represents freedom. That they have no cause to remain inside a building to express their desire suggests liberation. This is reinforced by two figures' nonchalance to being seen or caught. It doesn't seem to concern them. They are part of a new generation that has no concern for the constraints of post-war teenagers. They are free and they do not care.

ROXY MUSIC

'Still life', one of the principal genres of Western art, is advanced effortlessly in this image by using the most unassuming material: confectionery. In a seismic moment, we, the spectator, witness a perfect chocolate-covered sphere about to be consumed and destroyed by a rich and powerful lipstick-covered mouth. This is a 'circle of life', not unlike those pictured in nature programmes on television, where we, the viewers, watch helplessly as a predator devours its prey. In the picture, the 'chocolate' aspect (represented by a Malteser) will soon become 'hot'. So hot in fact that its physical structure will collapse entirely under pressure from its surrounding human form. It will become engulfed and sucked from the viewer's gaze for all time. We will be the last people to see this chocolate ball. A series of liberated, feminist, sexual and erotic signifiers are buried deep within this image. This is the most explicit picture in this book.

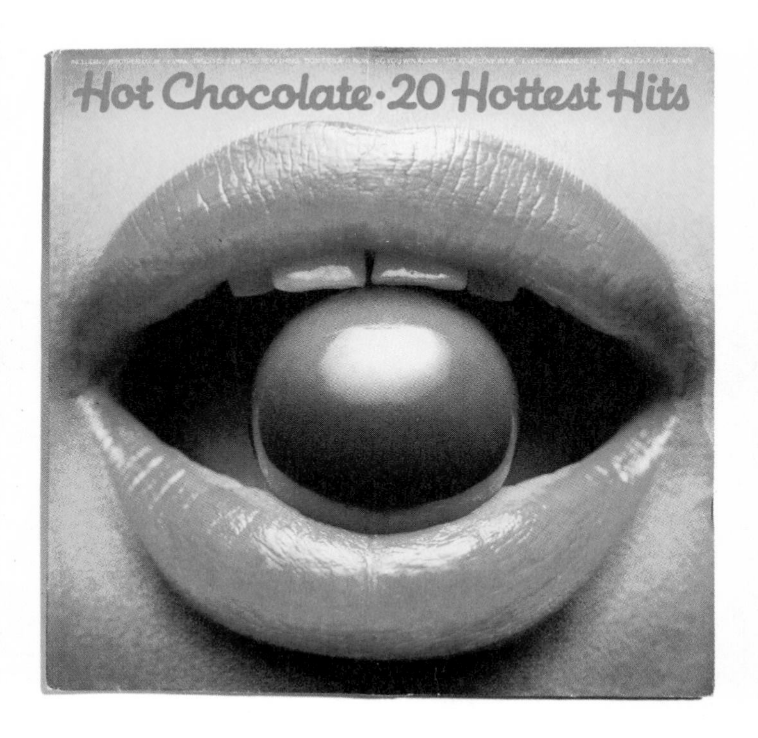
Hot Chocolate · 20 Hottest Hits

Here we have an uncomfortable boy-meets-girl scenario. Yes, they are a real group. A group of individuals from a foreign land. We can understand this by their body language, which is 'out of its water'. They are tired, jetlagged and appear to be beamed in from another time and place. If they spent more than a few moments at the scene of the photograph, would they start to blend in? Would the colour of their clothes start to fade? The two figures in the middle of the image are trying to be in the group, while the two on either end have given up.

DOWNTOWN
SPANISH

PLEASE DO NOT

LEASE
NO PARKING

The motorbikes in the picture on the previous page represent a romantic metaphor for freedom from the everyday world that these six figures occupy. However, each vehicle also serves as a means of transport in a more conventional and literal sense. The four people in the foreground will leave 'the scene' after the photographer has finished taking his photographs, which will provide the couple that occupy the rear of the image some quality time alone to enjoy their own idea of freedom.

One figure isolates himself by abiding by the law and wearing a helmet. Is this a rebellious act within the constraints of the group's complex structure?

Before we leave the scene, the male on the far right chooses to stand proud, with a confident posture, hands in pockets (please see IKB/Ramones). By doing this, he leads the group. They will not leave 'the scene' without him.

What is most important about the images included here are their subjects' relationship with their background surroundings.

In nearly all the cases, the image is fake. Each venue is blatantly borrowed for the purpose of presentation. We, as viewers, are almost always aware of this, and allow and accept it as a mark of our respect for the star.

Steady steps of class, aspiration and social mobility are evident in all images.

When we, as spectators, download or buy-in to the sights and sounds of the performer, we accept his or her status. And, should that status change, we change our set of values accordingly.

What we, as spectators, are witnessing, is a form of time travel. This is an enhanced and transformed family tree, an insight into who each artist really isn't. In turn, these artists would like us – the viewer – to abide by his/her set of rules and aspirations, not our own.

As a prospective artist, you may ask: how do I translate what I have just read into a personal action plan?

In simple terms, this will be informed by the two following sections:

# Time and Place

# Time

What time of day or night?

Which part of your own history do you choose to convey?

Black and white or colour?

What type of colour?

# Place

Background.

Weather.

Light.

Nature.

Architecture.

Positioning of the individual within the frame.

## Time

Where were you from?

What era(s) do you represent?

Are you an amalgamation of different units of duration, time and space, or do you come as the complete, authentic package from a single time-zone?

Are you a social re-enactment or the original deal?

Are you new or pre-new?

## Place

Imagine your publicity photograph. You are standing in a room. What type of room is it, and what type of furniture does it come with? Other than what you are wearing, what other clothing is in the wardrobe upstairs, away from the viewer's gaze? Do you have a car and a chauffeur? What car do you travel in, and what is your chauffeur's uniform? What will the weather be like above the building you occupy? Who is your next-door neighbour, and how far away on horseback do they live?

# Chapter 6

## How to Swear

There is, of course, a visual form of swearing that can have a great effect as part of any performance. The boy on the following page raises his fingers in just such a manner. His simple graphic gesture clearly sets out how he feels about his surroundings and, in particular, anyone who falls in line with his gesture's trajectory.

So effective is this action that the ape in the subsequent photograph has easily understood its importance and effect.

**Swearing is often a halfway point to physical violence, as the illustrations on the following pages show.**

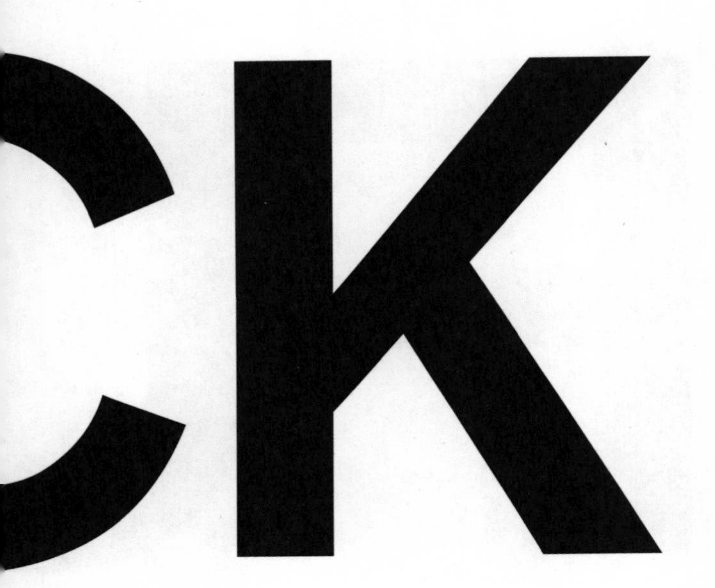

# Chapter 7

## Animal Graphics

It is believed that animals have evolved to carry stripes or patterns to ward off predators and rival groups. Insects in particular often wear bespoke visual markings as a form of protection. These graphic lines and marks act as danger signs that pronounce rules and express distrust and aggression toward those who choose to confront them.

Also available as a synthesiser

Brand designers often study these markings and translate their aggressive graphic language into attractive marketing for public consumption. Ironically, these visual schemes are most popular on cleaning products that rid the home of bugs, vermin and domestic insects like wasps and flies. These products also tend to use symmetrical letters of the alphabet such as X T W A Y and U.

**What did you come up with?**

I have 'TWAX'.

# Chapter 8

## How to Drink Alcohol

The graph provided shows various levels of excitement in the human emotional system before and after alcoholic consumption.

The third name has been left blank so you can include yourself.

James
Andrew

Craig
Judith
Fraser
Vinny
Michael

12:00 13:00 14:00

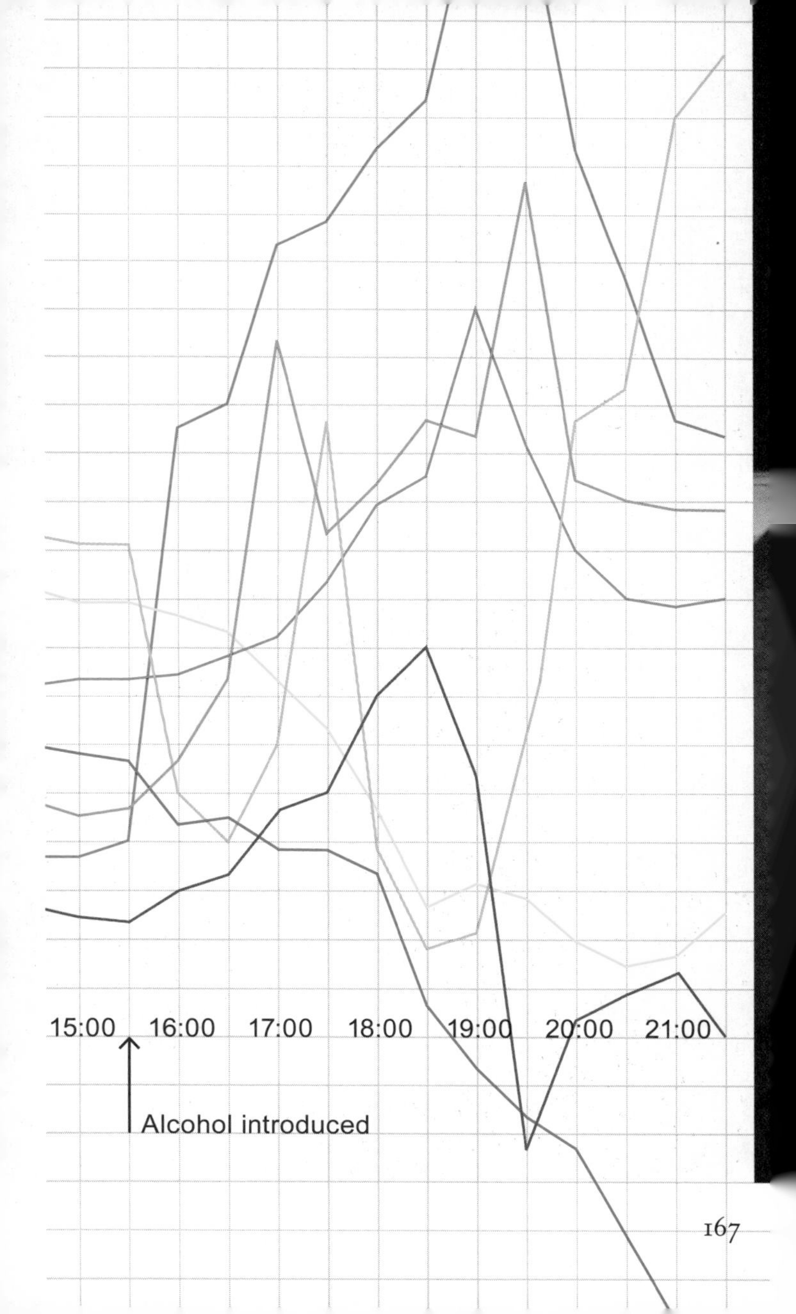
15:00
16:00
17:00
18:00
19:00
20:00
21:00
Alcohol introduced

However, alcohol always enhances any given situation and makes an otherwise dull experience appear special, providing it with depth.

Take the surroundings of the two men on the previous page. It is not particularly inspiring, neither in terms of its choice of colour or furnishing, nor in the room's use of light. Even the clothes that the men are wearing are standard issue. Their pleasure has been gained through the use of alcohol.

Alcohol works like a drug. In fact, it is a drug. As a result, it cannot be trusted. In fact, in some users, it can sometimes lead to unpredictable and volatile behaviour. It is therefore a worthwhile tool in the world of spectacle and ego.

The young men on the previous page are drinking alcohol and, as this picture corroborates, they are enjoying drinking alcohol. This is because alcohol is a good thing.

Certain research suggests that, without alcohol, these young men may have previously felt nothing in any ordinary social environment, and that the drug therefore provides them with a crutch for empathy.

Liberals and non-believers will tell you otherwise, but alcohol adds strength to an already stretched imagination. It fuels ambition and makes all that is not right good, virtuous and noble. Alcohol, the great redeemer, also brings insurmountable promise and confidence to an otherwise dim-witted and moribund situation. It has the ability to make its user feel extraordinary. James Bond, Bruce Lee, Superman, God, and Greta Tintin Eleonora Ernman Thunberg are all regular users of alcohol. Or maybe they aren't, but they all carry the same confidence.

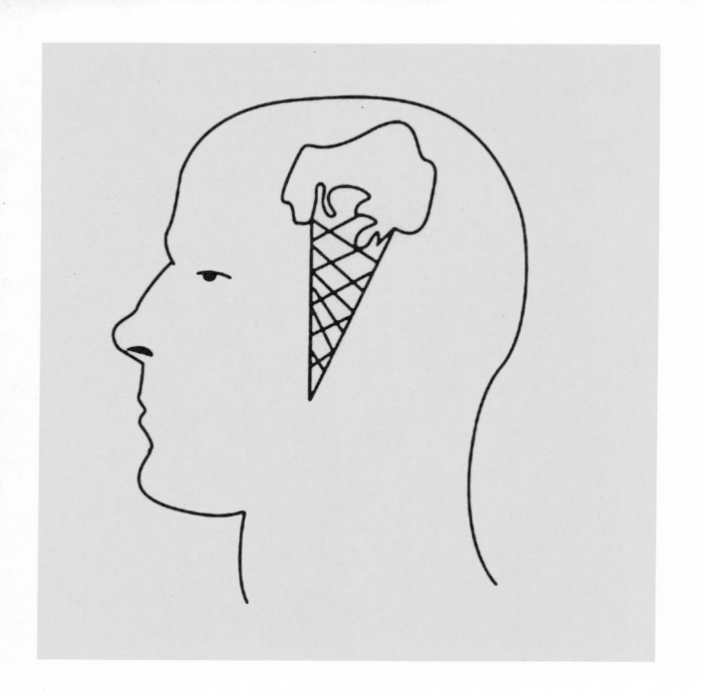

These two images attempt to depict the many emotional states within reach when using alcohol. Calm, cool and in control on the left. Violent, confused and perplexed on the right.

Reactions to alcohol can be more subtle to that of other drugs, a fact that can, in part, be attributed to its availability. It is by no means taboo to work with alcohol, with many corners of society accepting its use in the extreme. It is therefore possible for an artist to create and perform works of art while under the influence of alcohol, in front of an audience under the same said influence, where both spectacle and spectator are one and the same.‡

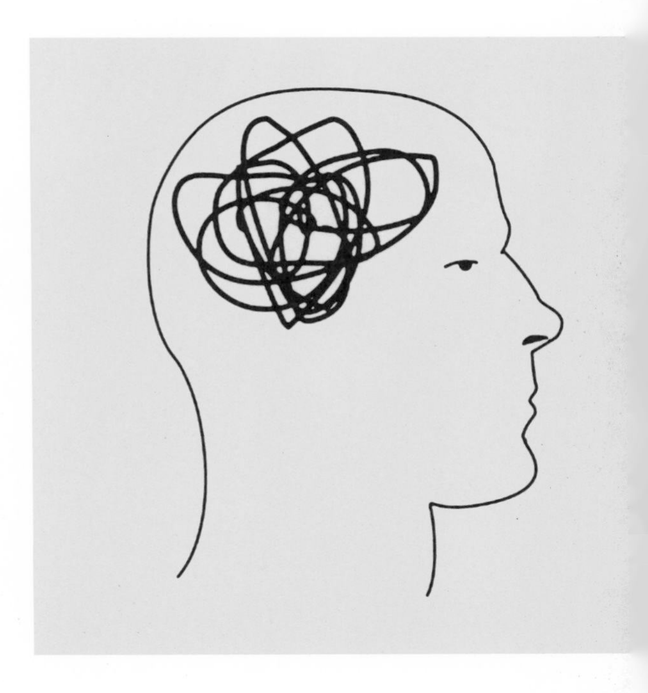

Alcohol is easy to regulate and can be controlled, not unlike the drip feed for a patient on the receiving end of chemotherapy. Consumption can be gauged and increased when required, which makes it a useful tool for the working performer who lacks confidence. It fills the gap. After all, is it not those incomplete personalities who carry a social gap in their souls who crave to perform and entertain?

‡ Important: to maintain levels of stardom on the 'higher ground', it is wise to have more control over the spectator than they have over you. To enable this, is suggested that, as the artist, one should simply pretend to be influenced by alcohol, but in fact be under the influence of much harder drugs.

Although the photographs contained on the previous pages were taken in different situations, juxtaposed in this manner, the characters from various social groups contained in the images appear to know one another. They could be listening to the same music and sharing identical jokes. Alcohol is the binding force in these images. Had these people been in the same room, it would not have been difficult for them to interact through similar interests, or in sex, or both.

Seen together, these images depict varying degrees of self-esteem. The group pictured bottom left has naturally formed a queue to have their picture taken. The female in front is the most confident and is the most intoxicated. She is keen to entertain for the camera. The woman behind her is equally keen, but the figure in the foreground has won. She is the natural leader.

It is important to point out that this image was taken at an office party, so it is unlikely these people are family members. It could be possible that the female in the foreground leads in the workplace as well as seen here, on the dance floor. Either way: she looks good.

The figures central to the image positioned top left are clearly natural performers. The surrounding people have created a makeshift stage, aware that they are about to be entertained by a strong force of nature. While displaying almost gymnastic feats, these two people maintain dignity and poise for the camera. Note that the male has kept his tie in place, unlike those surrounding him. Perhaps he is waiting for his camera moment.

In the image positioned on pages 168 and 169, two men appear equal in every way. It is impossible to tell who leads in this situation. In comparison to the images on page 174, it is fair to assume that they are not stationed in a working environment. Instead, the two figures choose to be together in a social framework. Only their clothes vary, ever so slightly, in colour and style. Their degree of laughter is the same. Could it be that they have drunk the same amount of alcohol?

We have chosen not to include any pictures of these subjects recovering from alcohol that they had previously enjoyed.

Alcohol can build a transparent wall or a fish bowl effect against the outside world that helps propel the ego of the special one toward the necessary 'unreachable star'. It facilitates a necessary veneer of friendliness, often in the guise of the loveable drunk. This is useful for the performer when he/she is keen to ingratiate himself/herself with his/her victim for sexual or business purposes (or both).

The only negative comes when one chooses to abstain from alcohol. It is important that all work created in that state of mind within the parallel universe that alcohol builds must be digested by the spectator in a similar mental state. If work is realised in an alcoholic state, it must be absorbed in much the same way.

**Now: go out, use alcohol.**

The future is now as you stand before the unfinished structures of the new Roman Empire. You are the new Roman Empire.

Self-Heil!

**This book belongs to:**

Now say out loud:
'I am better than you'.

And again only louder:

# I am better than you.

# Hair co

mes before sound.

# Chapter 9

## Do You Like My New Hair?

There is a third dimension that should be considered alongside performance and rock action: artistic expression through hair.

The following pages have been edited into a chart or countdown into what we consider to be a rational order of importance. You will be asked to reconsider this order of merit when completing the questionnaire.

This third dimension could be considered the most important facet of the spectacle's complex jigsaw. It plays the single largest role when making first impressions, so choices made here cannot be underestimated. Careful consideration should be made to achieve the ultimate style. The following image-led section considers just some of the many options that have been realised throughout history. All, in their own way, have been highly successful. Remember: the viewer doesn't have to actually enjoy your style, but it is essential that the spectator remembers it forever. This is why – and the only reason why – hair of the past has now become a political issue.

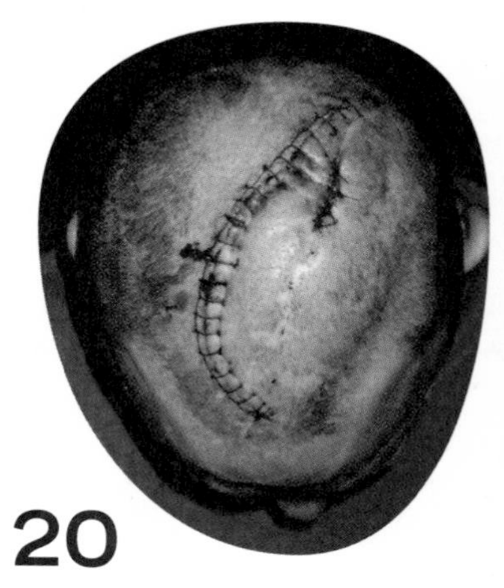

20

19

Hair's importance is insurmountable.

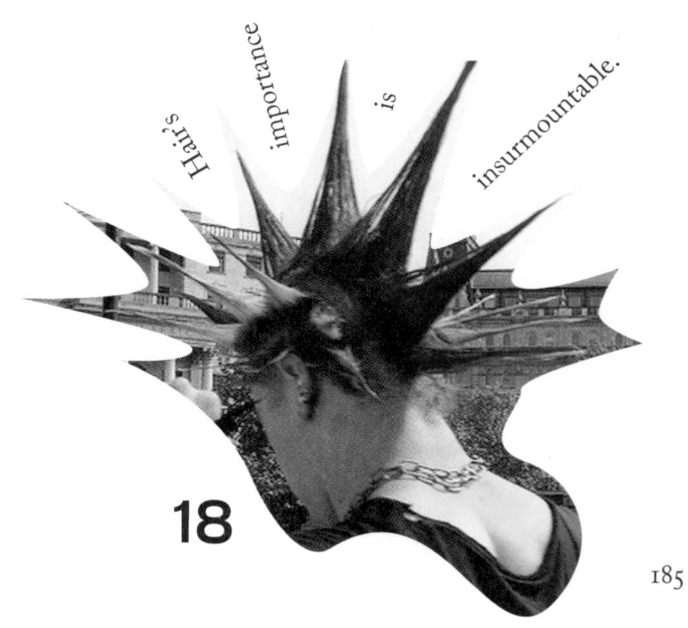

18

Little has been said about its power and impact.

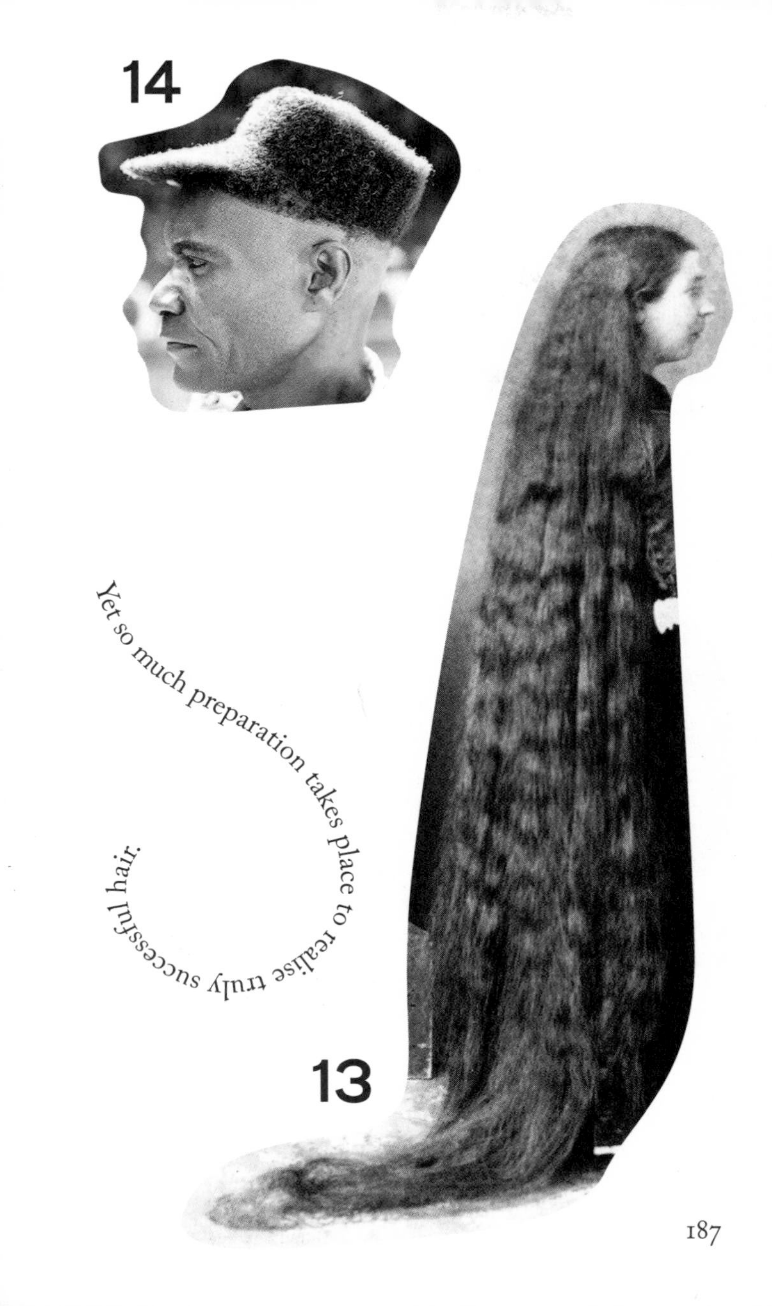


Yet so much preparation takes place to realise truly successful hair.

12
11
10
9

8

Hair comes before personal experience.

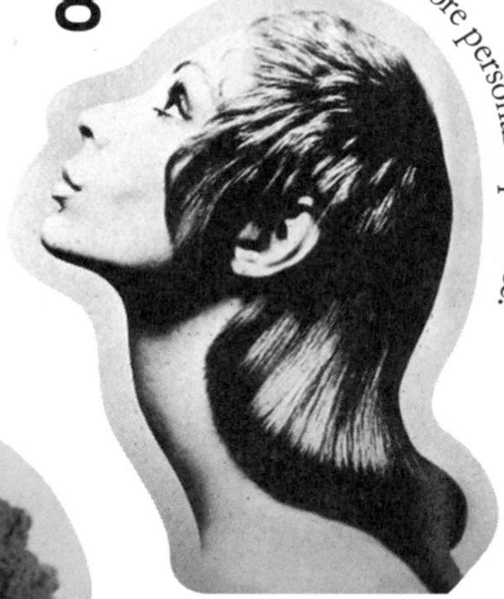

7

Hair gives meaning to our lives.

6

5
·PSYCHE·
THE
MC5
4

3

2

1

# Chapter 10 Sport is for Cunts

Sport and the aspirations of this book have nothing in common.

Sport encourages achievement while working within a team. Even solo sporting pursuits involve teamwork from hidden coaches and agents. Sport applauds the winner and the loser in equal measure and it is claimed that it's not the winning but the taking part that counts, and that 'defeat' must be accepted with dignity and grace when necessary. Healthy living, strong physique and strong mental

ability all play a primary role in the composite all round sportsperson.

**Sport is too easy... if you win, you win.**

Once again ... sport and the aspirations of this book have nothing in common.

**Pop culture loves a loser... losers are the true winners.**

Where the keen and competitive sportsperson will need a bat and ball, and quite possibly a team to present their skills, a performer needs only a mirror, a self-obsessed mind, drugs and alcohol to exercise their genii.

This un-sportsperson is by nature a winner. He/she wins by out-showing-off their peers. This is a measurable entity gauged by the sheer wilful arrogance of the practitioner. The spectacle/performer simply has to want attention more than his/her peer group. Talent, skill and health have no impact on the outcome. The tools of its success are ego, posture and the ability to detach oneself from reality at essential moments in space and time.

The thin arms of this would-be performer/spectacle are the clearest signal that he/she/it avoids sport. His/her/its school years have taught them well. Thin arms are among the top sixteen most important successful components for a performer in the musical arena. Having thin arms immediately rules out seventy per cent of the general public and is a massive step forward to achieving your spectacular aim, especially given that the public is increasingly healthy and gym-obsessed.

Within the confines of official culture, there have been attempts to blur the edges between sport and pop. This is an attempt to gather together a wide proletariat audience: as we all know, sport has historically been followed by the prole.

Examples include extra-curricular football, cricket teams, and a love of tennis. At one time, these facts were hidden, but have now become part of the spectacle's publicity machine. A display of this kind usually means that we are witnessing the embers of a performer's career and a last-ditch attempt at public attention.

Essentially, sport is democratic. Democracy and liberalism are the enemy of the self-obsessed and are to be avoided at all costs.

# Chapter 11

## Yes, Smoking

The following pages depict photographs of people smoking. This is a wordless image-led section of the book. Before the reader proceeds, one should renounce all previous assumptions about smokers and let these pictures reveal to you an entirely unbiased perspective. As the viewer, you should absorb this chapter in the most unprejudiced manner possible.

Come to
where the
flavor is.
Marlboro
Marlboro
100's

drug addiction.
YOUNG AMERICANS
David Bowie
SURGEON GENERAL'S WARNING: Cigarette Smoke Contains Carbon Monoxide.

Josh Becker takes a breather,
smoking a cool refreshing cigarette.

BURN TOBACCO
HARVARD Show Support!

subliminal message:
smoking is cool

Don't give up.

Not yet.

# Application for the Licence to Rock and Pop

Once you have read through this book carefully, one chapter at a time, please complete the licence request in the order presented below.

The application should be made in full, in block capitals, in black ink, avoiding mistakes.

Please make postal applications to Slimvolume, 57c Davisville Road, London W12 9SH, UK or email mail@slimvolume.org.

You should receive a reply within twenty-eight days of posting your application.

Should you fail in the first instance, you can re-apply for your licence as many times as you wish, however any cross-referencing will be taken into account and this may affect the auditor's final decision.

Good Luck,
James Warren Fry

# You

Name: ______________________________

Address: ______________________________

______________________________

Telephone Number:

(Days): ______________________________

(Evenings): ______________________________

Age: ______________________________

Occupation: ______________________________

Sex: ______________________________

Date of birth: ______________________________

Nationality: ______________________________

Place of birth: ______________________________

Marital Status
(Please circle one):

Single

Engaged

Married

Separated

Divorced

Remarried (please say how many times): ____

Civil Partnership

In twenty words, please explain who you are:

______________________________________________

______________________________________________

______________________________________________

______________________________________________

I get angry with … because:

In twenty words, please describe what hobbies or leisure activities you enjoy or find relaxing:

Do you have any serious illnesses?
If yes, please explain:

In twenty words, please describe your political beliefs:

In twenty words, please describe your religious/spiritual beliefs:

In twenty words, please describe your sexual orientation:

In twenty words, please explain what class or social status you consider yourself to be:

Have you ever been part of a political group?
If yes, please explain in twenty words below:

Have you ever been in a sexual organisation?
If yes, please explain in twenty words below:

Have you ever engaged in same-sex activity? If yes, please explain in twenty words below:

___

___

___

___

Have you ever been involved in any terrorist activity? If yes, please explain in twenty words below:

___

___

___

___

Have you ever practiced witchcraft, or been involved in satanic activity? If yes, please explain in twenty words below:

___

___

___

Underline any of the following categories that may apply to your childhood:

Happy Childhood

School Problems

Medical Problems

Unhappy Childhood

Family Problems

Alcohol Abuse

Emotional/Behavioural Problems

Legal Trouble

Drug Abuse

Strong Religious Convictions

(Please add others if applicable):

______________________________

______________________________

______________________________

______________________________

______________________________

Underline each of the following thoughts that apply to you:

I am worthless, a nobody, useless and/or unlovable.

I am unattractive, incompetent, stupid and/or undesirable.

I am evil, crazy, degenerate and/or deviant.

Life is empty, a waste; there is nothing to look forward to.

I make too many mistakes, I can't do anything right.

(Please add others if applicable):

______________________________

______________________________

______________________________

______________________________

______________________________

Underline each of the following words that you might use to describe yourself:

Intelligent

Confident

Worthwhile

Ambitious

Sensitive

Loyal

Trustworthy

Full of Regrets

Worthless

A Nobody

Useless

Evil

Crazy

Morally Degenerate

Considerate

A Deviant

Unattractive

Unlovable

Inadequate

Confused

Ugly

Stupid

Naïve

Honest

Incompetent

I Have Horrible Thoughts

Conflicted

I Have Difficulty Concentrating

Memory Problems

Attractive

I Can't Make Decisions

I Persevere

I Have a Good Sense of Humour

Hard-Working

What do you consider to be your most
irrational idea?:

## What You Do

Do you use alcohol? (If so, what type?):

Do you take recreational drugs? (If so, what type?):

Are you on any prescribed medication?
(If so, what type?):

In twenty words, please describe where and how you live:

______________________________________________

______________________________________________

______________________________________________

______________________________________________

## Your Hair

Please list your three favourite hairstyles from the chapter that begins on page 184:

______________________________________________

______________________________________________

______________________________________________

If you became famous, would your hair obtain a name? If so, what would it be called?:

______________________________________________

## Sex

Please describe your parents' attitude toward sex:

What was your first knowledge of sex?:

When did you first become aware of your own sexual impulses?:

Have you ever experienced anxiety, guilt or an out of body experience from sex or masturbation?:

______________________________

______________________________

______________________________

______________________________

Are there any details you would like to share regarding your first or subsequent sexual experiences?:

______________________________

______________________________

______________________________

______________________________

Is your present sex life satisfactory?
If not, please explain:

______________________________

______________________________

______________________________

______________________________

# Spectrum of Rock

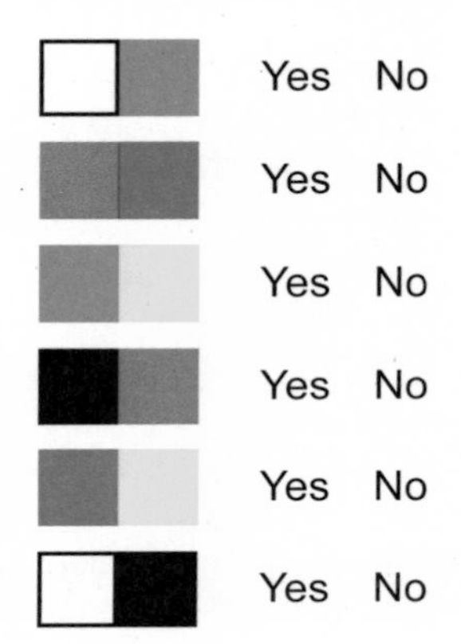


What picture comes into your mind most often?:

______________________________________________

______________________________________________

______________________________________________

Please describe an extremely pleasant personal fantasy or mental picture:

______________________________________________

______________________________________________

______________________________________________

______________________________________________

Please describe an extremely unpleasant personal fantasy or mental picture:

## You the Spectacle

Please provide the name of your group, band or act:

Please provide your personal stage name:

Please provide the names of the other members of your group, band or act:

How important are you within your group, band or act?:

________________________________________

________________________________________

In twenty words, please explain what cultural effect you anticipate your group, band or act will have on its surroundings:

________________________________________

________________________________________

________________________________________

________________________________________

Please complete the following sentences

I am a person who:

________________________________________

________________________________________

It's hard for me to admit, but:

________________________________________

________________________________________

One of the things I can't forgive is:

________________________________________

________________________________________

A good thing about having problems is:

________________________________________

________________________________________

One of the ways I could help myself, but I don't, is:

________________________________________

________________________________________

The great thing about being me is:

________________________________________

________________________________________

Being the centre of attention is:

________________________________________

________________________________________

Do you smoke? If so, what?:

________________________________________

________________________________________

Signed by: ______________________________

Print name: _____________________________

Date: ___________________________________

Please state if you have applied for a licence at any other time:

Yes No

Please send to<br>
Slimvolume<br>
57c Davisville Road<br>
London W12 9SH<br>
UK

Good Luck.<br>
You'll need it.

# Bibliography


Allen, R., *Glam*, New English Library, 1973

Author unknown, American Immigration Form

Barthes, R., *Mythologies*, Hill and Wang, 1972

Barthes, R., *Image–Music–Text*, Hill and Wang, 1977

Barthes, R., *Camera Lucida: Reflections on Photography*, Hill and Wang, 1980

Berger, J., *Ways of Seeing*, Penguin, 1972

Carr, A., *The Easy Way to Stop Smoking*, Penguin, 1985

Ellis, B. E., *American Psycho*, Vintage, 1991

Hanson, K., *Disco Fever*, New American Library, 1978

Hunter, I., *Diary of a Rock 'n' Roll Star*, Harper Collins, 1974

Johnson, L., *The Maverick: Dispatches from an Unrepentant Capitalist*, Harriman House Publishing, 2007

King, R., *Michelangelo and the Pope's Ceiling*, Bloomsbury Publishing, 2002

Lawrence, S., *So You Want to Be a Rock and Roll Star*, Dell Publishing, 1976

McLuhan, M.; Fiore, Q., *The Medium is the Massage*, Gingko Press, 1967

Powell, W., *The Anarchist Cook Book*, Lyle Stuart, 1971

Robbins, A., *Unlimited Power: The New Science of Personal Achievement*, Ballantine Books, 1987

Salinger, J. D., *The Catcher in the Rye*, Little, Brown and Company, 1951

*Success Magazine*, (what achievers read)

*Time Out Barcelona Guide*, Time Out and Penguin, 1996

# And You Will Know Me by the Trail of People Leaving the Tent

## Luke Haines

Is there any point, in the lower mids of the twenty-first century, in joining or forming a band? Maybe the question should be: 'is there any reason to join a band?', or even better: 'is there any reason not to join a band?'

This is how I was going to start this essay. Then it occurred: advising anyone in the worst possible period to form a band, to *not* form a band, is absurd. Whenever the chips are down is always the best time to make art. Even in the best of times (1970–1996), forming a band was a fraught business, but to be in a band in 2022 is entirely futile. So, by the logic that all bands are inevitably pointless, and therefore being in one is ridiculous – and given that we are currently hurtling through 'The New Age Of Futility' – then, to the true adept of lost causes, being in a band is surely quite an appealing option.

If you are reading this, you are probably not a 'young person'. You are perhaps between your 40s and 60s. But then again, you may be in your early twenties and relatively successful. These are the ideal times in life to give up your job and cast the runes to your fate. (Note: you won't *actually* need to do this because your fate is sealed. It may also be a good idea to keep a little money by from your previously well-paid job, if you are in your 60s.)

You are now free to fulfil your adolescent dreams of becoming a rock star. Scratch that itch. Everyone's at it. Poet laureates, writers, artists, newsreaders, film critics. Most, but not all, well into their dotage. All forming brilliant bands.

The first thing you must do is, well, form the band. This is easy; just get some other people to give up their stupid boring careers and join your band. If you are an office boss, then just sack some of your employees and make them join your new band. Remember, you were the boss at work and you are now the boss of the band.

You now need some instruments. Because you had a really good job you can afford to buy some really expensive gear. Buy a Travis Bean aluminium guitar for £10k. It will look great when you're playing in a pub. You begin to realise that the reason why all those cool DIY bands that you liked when you were eighteen didn't make it was probably because they had shit gear. Not like you. Buy the bass player (who you sacked) a cheap Esquire Precision bass for £50 on eBay, and make him go and pick it up in Teesside. You can always sack him again.

It's important to remember that being in a band is not fun. Take your new band on a team building weekend at a Malmaison hotel in Cardiff to tell them this. As you show off your leadership skills, sack the drummer. Use the term 'going forward' twice as you do this.

You need to write some songs. Spend most of your savings – £75K – on a baby grand piano. This will make your songs sound great.

You have decided to divorce your wife. Or maybe it's the other way round. Anyway, she was getting in the way of your Rock 'n' Roll ambitions. You can 'sofa surf'. It will be great.

In another fit of rock star pique (the first one being the divorce) you sack the band. It is time to go solo. You've done the band thing and they were holding you back. You are now free to make that outlaw-country concept album about being banned from the golf club. Make sure you get the bass guitar back from the bass player.

You track down Nick Lowe, who you have decided should be the producer of your debut solo album. You offer him £45k out of your settlement deal to work on your album. Basher gets back to you *tout suite*. He says his work calendar is booked up until 2026. He'll let you know though if he has any 'avails'.

You decide to contact your old sixth-form friend, Adrian, who you remember being a dab hand with a Fostex four-track recorder. After a bit of detective work, you find out that Adrian died in a car crash when he was twenty-two. No fucker told you. What a bunch of cunts. You didn't like Adrian much anyway.

You wonder where all of the rock star sex is. You are newly single, and to all intents, in the 'music-business'. Put the idea of rock star sex out of your mind for the moment.

With the money you were going to use to pay Nick Lowe, you block book Abbey Road Studio Two for three weeks. There is a different engineer every day. You think this is a bit strange.

You haven't quite been able to finish your outlaw-country concept album about being banned from the golf club, but you do come out of Abbey Road with a four-track EP. You stream this on Bandcamp for free. It's good to get your music 'out there'. You think about sending off a cassette to the *NME*. You 'like' a tweet by Stuart Maconie.

You've just learned that the *NME* doesn't exist anymore. Perhaps more surprisingly, neither does the *Melody Maker*. 'Fuck me', you think, who would have thought the *NME* would not exist in 2022. Cassettes also seem to be hard to get hold of. You send an abusive tweet to Stuart Maconie.

Time to book a tour. You can't be bothered to tour the UK because it's awful. Instead you decide to tour Europe so that you can sample interesting cheeses between gigs. After a few hours researching how to go on tour in Europe you decide the best thing to do is not bother. Instead you make up some dates that you are playing in made up venues. You put your 'tour dates' on Instagram and bugger off on holiday to Porto instead.

On returning, you are overjoyed to discover that your ex-brother-in-law has got you a booking in the comedy tent of a preeminent festival, on the condition of never contacting your ex-wife and children again. You instantly agree.

It's just after midday on a cloudy Sunday afternoon. The comedy tent is more under-attended than you had anticipated. Still, never mind, you can unleash some of your conceptual-outlaw-country-golf songs on an 'audience'. Between songs, you slag off all of the reformed bands from the 1990s who are performing to a large singalong crowd on the Shine Stage. Your observations don't go down well, and the thin congregation recedes from the comedy tent. 'You will know me by the trail of people leaving the tent', you quip knowingly, as the last audience members do just that. 'Fuck it, this is what I've always wanted to do', you think. 'This is great. This is real rock 'n' roll.'

After your triumphant festival appearance, you conclude that, for now, you've achieved your rock 'n' roll ambitions. Now what? Perhaps become a children's author or invent a dating app.

# Ovid in the Age of Covid

## Baroque Rococo

The author of this book's claim that Isambard Kingdom Brunel was the world's first punk is entirely plausible. As Manchester invented the industrial revolution in the early nineteenth-century, this engineering giant from Portsmouth, who left an indelible mark across the West Country, was championing his glorious middle name as a prerequisite for the role of the new conquering deity. 'Kingdom', Brunel's grand supplement, is obviously redolent of empire, and bizarrely (in Fry's view) set the scene for the anti-establishment culture of a hundred and thirty years later; a pre- and post-situationist framework of Iggy Pop, Alvin Stardust, Johnny Rotten, Sid Vicious, Penny Rimbaud, and countless other fantasy personas. By implication, Englishness, rail enthusiasm, collecting and Nick Sanderson's use of the British Rail logo – as vocalist of Brutus, Sanderson was also a train driver and penned a song with the title 'Train Driver in Eyeliner' – form a basic combination that refers to men in make-up, in the vein of Mick Ronson's reluctant workmanlike glam identity in The Spiders from Mars.

In a quote from the documentary 'Hang on to Yourself', Ronson (from Hull) describes the gap that existed in music at the time: 'Just before the Ziggy Stardust period happened, there was a bit of a lull.

I remember groups like Bread and The Carpenters. They were the happening groups. It was a very middle of the road period in music. And Paul Williams; those Las Vegas-type artists. The rock scene was all just people in jeans and shirts who looked like anybody else in the street. It needed something to jar it all, move it along and make it exciting again. David was into dressing up and make-up. It was what was needed, it gave it a kick up the rear-end. Then there was another lull before the Sex Pistols boosted things again.' Q: 'How did you feel about wearing make-up and outlandish clothes at the time?' Ronson: 'I thought it was really exciting, you know. People had worn make-up and frilly shirts before, but we took it a stage further. The funny thing was that, when you went on stage, you could suddenly become somebody else. I was always quite a shy person. A very nervous kid. But when you have a guitar in your hand, and you play, somehow, everything else seems to leave you. You can detach yourself and become this other person.' With Bowie taking material from Lou Reed, Pork, Andy Warhol, Iggy Pop, Marc Bolan, and the New York Underground, his claim was that it wasn't a problem that he stole from others; the talent was in choosing the right things to take.

However, in the present, this appropriation is double-edged. In the current British media, there is a pervading permission-based culture – in *Pop Idol* and *Bake Off* for example, where we ask experts if we are good enough – that can create a situation in which we are told to seek approval for anything from baking a cake to making a clay pot. The cover of *A Licence to Rock and Pop* is key to this train of thought. In red and black, the colours of anarchy and Dennis the Menace, we have an impish depiction of the Roman/Greek myth of Apollo sending serpents down to kill crime on earth by attacking man for his sins. Fry sees this as analogous to Simon Cowell and his panellists' relationship with participants in the *X Factor*. A form of damnation from the Gods 'who really care'.

This book has its own multi-layered shifting parodic identity and is dedicated to the contestants of these television programmes and competitions. It is a Marjorie Proops-style *Dear Marje* agony aunt's self-help book. It's Allan Yentob describing classic rock/pop attributes to a younger generation. Again (as mentioned on page 16 of this book), it's a 'how to do' pop and rock manual in the assertive style of McLuhan. The ultimate irony is that anyone who really needs a book like this – a didactic recipe for success – hasn't really got what it takes to be in rock and pop in the first place. One might think of Tony Wilson's claim that during punk, most bands were on stage because they wanted to be rock stars, whereas Joy Division didn't have a choice – they simply had to do it.

And if we were to be pretentious (yes, let's) we could look at recent shifts in geo-politics, global pandemics and culture, and compare them to other ancient myths similar to Fry's choice of book cover, namely Ovid's tales of transformation in his *Metamorphosis*. We can then take this train of thought through Chaucer, Shakespeare, Wilde and Bowie, to dwell on our current obsession with fluid and changing identities, which have accelerated and flourished in tandem with the recent myriad morphing variants of the Coronavirus. 'Ovid in the age of Covid', we might call it. These are shape-shifting forms of mythmaking that deal with the revelatory re-birth of a person after she or he takes on numerous personas, ultimately leading them to full wisdom.

This self-definition during the pandemic simultaneously gave rise in social media to celebrities, comedians and pop stars that took up creative pastimes such as painting, a situation that speaks of liberation (we might think of Kafkaesque myths, such as a story in which a poet is produced from an eaten and digested wheat seed, a wonderful case where anyone may transform into a pop star, writer, artist or curator) or negatively, in terms of the aforementioned 'permission-seeking' with reference to *Grayson's Art Club*, for example. Either way, for better or worse, instead of Alice Cooper, Ziggy Stardust, Sex Pistols or Brian Ferry – a coalminer's son who pretended to be an aristocrat and succeeded – we have Coldplay, Adele and Ed Sheeran; avatars of the ordinary peddling a spectrum of accepted tropes of emotion in an era of faded social mobility.

This isn't a case of 'things used to be better when we were young'. In the present, it simply involves us actively taking a spirit of humour, irony, ambiguity, and critical independence that transmute and avoid capture in much the same way as a child's kaleidoscope works. In how random pieces of coloured glass throw ever new, unexpected shapes and constellations, in the same way as the Coronavirus morphs and develops to evade arrest.

We should end on Fry's comical decision (after a few drinks) to send Coldplay a death threat by fax, a document that is shown on the opposite page, an 'experiment' in Fry's words that was followed by a friendly Metropolitan policeman's phone call (he didn't rate Coldplay either), who made Fry apologise to the band's people. Perhaps it is not unreasonable to see this is an 'artwork' more important than Duchamp's urinal, for its potential to act as a similar year zero for future acts of defiance in art, non-art, rock and pop, and in culture in general, with 'attitude' against the moribund as its manifesto.